Hope's Motive

Hope's Motive

Ben Fisher

Why Publishing

Copyright © 2021 by Ben Fisher

All rights reserved. No part of this book may be reproduced in any manner whatsoever without written permission except in the case of brief quotations embodied in critical articles and reviews.

First Printing, 2021

ISBN: 978-1-8383531-2-4

Unless otherwise stated, Scripture quotations are from the ESV® Bible (The Holy Bible, English Standard Version®), copyright © 2001 by Crossway, a publishing ministry of Good News Publishers. Used by permission. All rights reserved.

Scripture quotations [marked NIV] taken from the Holy Bible, New International Version Anglicised Copyright © 1979, 1984, 2011 Biblica

Used by permission of Hodder & Stoughton Ltd, an Hachette UK Company.

All rights reserved.

'NIV' is a registered trademark of Biblica UK trademark number 1448790.

Hope's Motive

Introduction

This short book on Hope has been extracted and edited from a larger one: The Who and The Why, which looks at faith, hope and love together. In that book, I argue that the most helpful way to label these three attributes, so highly valued in the bible, is as 'motivational characteristics.' That is to say, that God wants to embed these three things at the core of our souls, to both define who we are, and motivate what we do. For it's not just what we do that's important, but why we do it. God has never been looking to simply change our actions, but rather to change us from the inside out – to alter our hearts and minds so that they naturally want and pursue all that is right and good.

God is constantly working in His adopted children to conform them more and more to the likeness of His Son, Jesus Christ. But this doesn't mean He's out to make us all a bunch of clones. God is far too creative for that, and besides, the infinite worth and wonder of Christ could never be captured in any single one of us. But consistent throughout each and every one of us is God's desire to embed in the core of our being a faith, hope and love, which is both sourced and sustained in God alone. These three attributes are of eternal value and will remain as relevant in the next life as they are now. This book takes on the topic of hope, seeking to understand what it is exactly, how it affects us, and how we can work alongside God as He grows it within us.

Building character?

Now let me ask you – have you ever been through a hard time and had someone say to you "cheer up – it's all character building"? Were you blessed by this? No – me neither. Which is why its frankly annoying to discover that it's actually very biblical, and I don't even mean that the principle can be found as you bring various truths together – it's right there out in the open and plain to see in the book of Romans: *"Therefore, since we have been justified by faith, we have peace with God through our Lord Jesus Christ. Through him we have also obtained access by faith into this grace in which we stand, and we rejoice in hope of the glory of God. Not only that, but we rejoice in our sufferings, knowing that suffering produces endurance, and endurance produces character..."[1]*

Yes, you read it right, that utterly annoying (and probably somewhat wonderful) Christian friend of yours was correct! Almost. But this sentence from scripture wasn't over:

> *"...Not only that, but we rejoice in our sufferings, knowing that suffering produces endurance, and endurance produces character, and character produces hope, and hope does not put us to shame, because God's love has been poured into our hearts through the Holy Spirit who has been given to us."*

Rom 5:3-5

Hope. Why is it that no one encourages us to 'cheer up' or rejoice during harder times because of the hope it can ultimately produce? Why do we so often keep a step back and just go with the more general term: character? I think part of the reason is a self-feeding one, in that we simply neither talk about nor value hope properly. And when we do it's in general airy-fairy terms. We're told that the greatest of these is love[2]. We can infer that the foundation of these is

---

1. Rom 5:1-4
2. 1 Cor 13:13

faith. And sadly, in my view, the most neglected is hope.

In this book, we will be exploring the nature and purpose of hope, the second of the main 'motivational characteristics', which God wants to embed in your soul, at the very core of who you are. In my experience hope is very rarely if ever taught directly about, whereas both faith and love are frequently talked about, and woven into other subjects. Maybe it's because hope is harder to pin down and talk about without coming across a little 'fluffy' and insubstantial? But the truth is without hope the soul withers, and in time gives birth to despair, which at its most extreme leads people to despair even of life itself. Hope is important!

The expectation of future good

We need to start by trying to define the hope we're talking about, as how the word is most frequently used is not the biblical concept of hope. The main way that we tend to use the word hope is in an expression of optimism, such as: "I hope that the weather will be good this weekend". But it may or may not be accompanied by any expectation of this happening (especially if you live in the unpredictable north of England as I do). So you may hear exactly the same phrase from someone who has no real belief that it will turn out good. In this case, it's not even optimism but merely an expression of desire. It's a wish.

So what does the Bible say to help us understand? Here we need to start with the simple and basic aspects, making sure we don't just rush over them because they seem too obvious. In doing so we find the truths which give us the right foundation needed to add more elements. Our main focus will be in Romans 5 where we started this chapter, but before we dive into that more deeply it will be helpful to skip ahead to something else the apostle Paul said in his letter to the Romans: *"...But hope that is seen is no hope at all. Who hopes for what they already have? But if we hope for what we do not yet have we wait for it patiently."*[3] Who hopes for what they already have? No one. The very nature of hope is to look to the future – to something we don't yet have, something good. For we could also ask the question "who hopes for something bad to happen to them". No one. That is unless despair has taken over hope's role in someone's life, and even then, the bad they're wishing for is because they believe it will ultimately help them feel better. So we can define hope as *the Expectation of Future Good.*

3. Rom 8:24-25 (NIV)

It's a definition that will probably surprise few people, but still it's helpful to pin down and state. These words have also been chosen carefully. Why 'expectation'? I've chosen to use this word as it allows for both certainty and vagueness, which as I'll try and show throughout this chapter is needed for a fully helpful definition of Hope. However, I must acknowledge straight away that I am treating this just slightly differently from anywhere else I've read about the original Greek. Pretty much everywhere I've read up about this has treated it as meaning an *assured* or *certain* expectation[4], making it more absolute and definitive than I'm doing.

Now bear with me, and let me try to briefly run through why I think this isn't quite right. In the classical Greek of the time "elpis/elpizo" (hope) in gentile use, was a personal projection of future events of all kinds, whether good or bad, but there was no certainty attached to it. Depending on the context, the word might actually have been used to describe fear instead of hope. So for many, the word meant something much broader and more subjective than how we tend to use the word. But for the Jews, because of the translation into Greek of their Hebrew scriptures, they were used to the word always being used positively, denoting confidence and trust (in God). So as we hit the New Testament we have

---

4. One example is: The NIV Theological Dictionary of New Testament Words, edited by Verlyn D. Verbrugge, Zondervan, 2000

people writing to others who are used to the word being used in a variety of ways, with a mixture of Jewish and gentile believers. Now it's here in the New Testament that the claim is made that 'hope' is always used of an assured expectation, and I would indeed agree that the hopes spoken of are indeed absolutely certain – usually. But not always. There are some places where to my mind it seems to be used in a looser way, such as Paul's expectation (not absolute certainty) of coming to visit the Corinthians:

> *"For I do not want to see you now just in passing. I hope to spend some time with you, if the Lord permits."*

1 Cor 16:7

Also, saying that most 'hopes' spoken of in the Bible are a certainty, is not the same thing as saying that hope itself carries or embodies the meaning of certainty. To my mind treating it this way becomes less helpful when considering hope's function more broadly.

Consider this from Hebrews:

> *"So when God desired to show more convincingly to the heirs of the promise the unchangeable character of his purpose, he*

> *guaranteed it with an oath, so that by two unchangeable things, in which it is impossible for God to lie, we who have fled for refuge might have strong encouragement to hold fast to the hope set before us. We have this as a sure and steadfast anchor of the soul, a hope that enters into the inner place behind the curtain, where Jesus has gone as a forerunner on our behalf, having become a high priest forever after the order of Melchizedek."*

Heb 6:17-20

Hope is an anchor for the soul, to keep us steady in turbulent times. But anchors don't always work, they can fail if not used properly or if the water is simply too deep. What makes this anchor so sure? What makes it unbreakable and long enough for any situation? Its God Himself. It's His perfect and unchanging character, it's His inability to lie, make a mistake, be surprised, or come up against a force even close to being greater than He is. If God has promised, then that is that, you can be absolutely sure of it, because you can be absolutely sure of Him.

Consider what the book of Hebrews has to say about faith: *"faith is the assurance of things hoped for, the conviction of things not seen"*[5]. Faith is about

5. Heb 11:1

certainty, but to consider hope, in the same way, makes this sentence a little redundant: "faith is the assurance of things you're certain of…". If you're certain about something you don't need assurance of it. You're either certain or you're not. And whilst we're here let's notice one more thing; it looks like the writer here is saying the same thing in two different ways to emphasise the point: assurance of hope, and conviction of things unseen. Assurance and conviction, hope and the unseen. So it affirms our earlier point that you don't hope for what you already have, but something that you don't – something unseen. Also, it starts to hint part of the way hope affects and motivates us – hope is linked to our sight or the way we view life, something we'll explore over the course of this book.

So hope's source and centre is where the certainty is; our unchanging God, what He's like and what He's said; Christ Jesus, what He's done, doing, and will yet do at His return. But hope's intended flow and function in our lives is both broader and vaguer than to label it as merely another word for certainty. Whereas faith is all about certainty, Christian hope stands on certainty, or to continue the sailing theme from before; hope's anchor is firmly sunk into the bedrock of an unchanging and awesome God. It's a subtle difference at first glance, but if we don't make the distinction we end up with faith by another name. And whilst our faith is amazing and irreplaceable, equally, we don't want faith to replace one of God's other gifts to us. Hope's function is more varied and life-giving than to simply be a comforter or a steadfast anchor during lives storms. Hope keeps us holding on and looking forward in the bad times, and keeps us looking up and moving forward in the good times, filling us with joyous anticipation.

Working on the production line

We return now to the part of Romans where we started this book, and Paul is getting excited. By now he has taken his readers through some hard-hitting truths about our nature and predicament before a just and righteous God, and in turn the incredible grace He has given to us through faith in Christ Jesus – making us right before God without compromising His justice. Building on this Paul now says because of this grace in which we now stand *"we rejoice in hope of the glory of God"*[6]. We look forward to the day when we'll see the glory of God, face to face – when we'll know God fully just as we are fully known to Him[7]. How incredible will that be! But "not

6. Rom 5:2
7. 1 Cor 13:12

only that", he says, *"we rejoice in our sufferings"*[8]. What?! Why on earth would we rejoice in our sufferings? Well Paul moves straight into explaining; suffering produces endurance – ok, I can see that, the old 'whatever doesn't kill you makes you stronger' type thing and you start to find that you can cope more? Then; endurance produces character – well yes, I guess I can say that I can see in my own life and others how enduring times of suffering has strengthened and built up character. And finally; character produces hope. Now, this last step isn't as immediately obvious as the others, but I believe the reason is this – our growth and building up in character is evidence of God's sanctifying work in us. Being able to see the results of God working these hard and difficult times into something of great worth – better character. This in turn produces hope, because we have the evidence right there in us of God truly with us, and at work bringing good fruit out of bad times. All of this serves to strengthen our foundation from which we expect God to do more good things in the future.

But please note – this process is not automatic. This production line which starts with suffering doesn't inevitably lead to hope. Indeed, not everyone comes out the other side better. Whereas some come through maybe more determined or caring; mentally

[8]. Rom 5:3

stronger or sympathetic, others come out bitter or hating; arrogant or self-seeking. Others still, come out entirely unchanged in terms of character. I wonder if the key doesn't lie in something else you can find in the book of Hebrews:

> *"For the moment all discipline seems painful rather than pleasant, but later it yields the peaceful fruit of righteousness to those who have been trained by it."*

Hebrews 12:11

Notice here that that the discipline from God, only results in good fruit for those who have been trained by it. I'm certain that God is working all sorts of stuff into our lives and characters without us realising it straight away, but there is an expectation on us to engage with what God is doing. The *out*-working of faith, hope and love, when they're already embedded in the core of our being, is an automatic and wonderful one – if they're there it'll just ooze out of you to some level without you even trying. However, the *working in* of these things takes time. It will require a more conscious surrender and working alongside God in His plans to see them established. So now when I'm in the middle of more difficult periods, I'm trying to remember to ask God to what it is that He wants to work into me through them? How is He trying to help me grow and develop, what good can be forged in this bad? (Alongside pleading that He'll get me out the other side quickly).

So when you're travelling through a darker time in life, take heart. For God will see you through to better times, whether in this life or the next. And if you're open to being trained by it, God will build up in you hope, a precious gift of more worth than words can describe.

The old familiar rod

Thankfully, God is a God of many means and methods, and suffering is not the only tool He uses to build up hope in our souls. As Paul says later in this same letter:

> *"For whatever was written in former days was written for our instruction, that through endurance and through the encouragement of the Scriptures we might have hope."*

Romans 15:4

Reading through God's interactions with His people recorded in the Bible has such potential to give us hope. So many different and flawed characters, just like us, for whom God stepped in and made the difference. As we read His Word, we can begin to understand How God deals with us, and His plans to release us from bondage to sin, so that we might instead be bound to Him. It's glorious, strengthening, hope enhancing stuff. But again, the process is not automatic. It is entirely possible to study the Bible hard, learn the background to all the different books within it, memorise vast portions, and yet have no real relationship with God. This is because it's not being treated as the all-authoritative word of God, and so sadly it doesn't build us up as it could. The Bible will not have its due impact on us if we don't come to it in faith that it is from God, and that He knows better than we do. We must come open and surrendered, doing our very best not to put our views on it, but instead letting It align our views with His. When we do, we're opening ourselves up to have this hope grown, encouraged and watered within us – along with many other good things.

Now the problem with talking about this is that it can feel like the old familiar rod coming back out to beat us up again, knowing as we do, that we should probably pray and read the Bible more. Isn't that the lesson we so often hear? And we've heard it so many times, that we tend to feel both guilty and numbed by the challenge. I hate thinking about how much of my life I've spent not being disciplined enough to make sure I set aside this sort of regular time with God. And then I move on from thinking about it because so much is going on which needs my attention. Or perhaps I simply feel the need to flop and do nothing for a bit, because I'm already so tired from everything else. Why is it, that bad habits are so easy to form but hard to stop; whereas good habits are hard to form and easy to stop?

As I said - the rod is hard to avoid when talking about this, and though many of us are already numb to it, if we're honest, we know full well that we need a bit of a prod to get us on track. But let me attempt to bring out both the 'carrot and the stick'. You probably know well the story of Mary and Martha. Jesus entering a village is welcomed by Martha into her home, where Jesus starts talking and teaching many things. Mary sits with the others listening, whilst her sister is busy getting food ready for everyone on her own – getting all the jobs done, whilst silently getting more and more annoyed with Mary for not helping. That is until she stops being silent and says: *"Lord, doesn't it bother you that my sister has left me to do all the work by myself? Tell her to come and help me!"*[9] But Jesus doesn't. As is so often the case He turns it around, and with care

9. Luke 10:40

pouring out, gently challenges Martha "...*You are worried and upset about many things, but only one thing is necessary. Mary has chosen what is best, and it will not be taken away from her*."[10] How difficult it is to judge this right. Because there many things that we truly do need to get done, and God would also admonish those who too easily let their responsibilities slide. But we can't just dismiss the challenge claiming that we simply have too much to do. That would be to ignore part of God's word by making excuses for ourselves. If we don't have time, then we're doing too much, and it's something else that should be let go off or reduced. If we can't 'fit God in' to our lives, then something is very wrong. Indeed, if we come at it with the mindset of simply trying to fit Him and His word in, then we're already coming at it with the wrong attitude.

There are two sentences I keep before me to challenge and encourage me in this area. The first is a book title: *'Too Busy Not To Pray'*, by Bill Hybels. I confess I've never read the book. Somehow, I've never felt the need to. Simply reading its title I get challenged and feel like nothing more needs to be said. It remains on my bookshelf as a reminder to not *make excuses*, but instead to *make time* for prayer, especially when I'm busy. I remember a phrase I heard a preacher use once: *'Feeding Leftovers To A*

10. Luke 10:41-42

Hungry God'. Wow does that pierce my heart at times. It's so easy to just fit God in around other things and give Him just the scraps of our day, or even week or month. Quite simply, if the way we arrange our days suggest that God is an add-on, a blessed extra when we can fit Him in, instead of the highest priority of our minds, then something is seriously wrong!

It can be really hard to get this right, and once you've got it right, somewhere down the road, you might have to change it to keep it right? As a wise man once said to me, *"you'll find that you need to keep re-learning the same lessons"*. And this is partly because circumstances change. This might be through getting married, having kids, changing jobs, or simply because your own physical or mental capabilities alter over time (for the better or worse). It might be that at one time, spending time with God late in the evening worked great for you, and you were alert and had good times. But slowly you've started to find that you're less switched on as it gets later in the day, so you need to either alter your routine or find new ways of making the most of that time.

In these things, we must support and help in each other, and it's worth asking yourself the question: "Can I be a Martha for a Mary sometimes?"

My wife and I do this most weekends. We both give the other one some time to spend alone with God, whilst the other person does jobs and looks after the children. This has been a good and helpful step forwards for us, as we've adjusted to the major life change of having two children added into our family.

Carrot hunting

Well, that's quite enough of the 'stick' for now, and this is not a book about getting our personal time with God sorted out. So let's briefly consider what 'carrots' are there to feast on. And it's quite simple really – it will do you good. I mean such incredible good! And you'll need to maintain it to truly know it's on-going benefits. But simply put, God has given us His Word, and granted us access into His presence, any place, any time, in order to bless us. We're missing out when we don't make time and prioritise Him in this way – and surely we don't want to miss out on such a great thing. I find the saying we take from the Bible that: *"the spirit indeed is willing, but the flesh is weak"*[11] to be all too true in me, especially in this kind of context (indeed the original context, is about the disciples failing to stay up and pray with Jesus). A part of me wants to, and the other part is

11. Matt 26:41

always trying to get out of it because it feels like too much effort. But whenever I win that battle, I'm always so pleased that I bothered to try and push through, and I can feel its worth. What's more, the busier I am, the greater my need of it, and so the more potential it has to prove itself fulfilling, and worth fighting for.

Why do it? Because God blesses us through it, and among other things, will use it to build us up in life-giving, God-exalting hope. That's a pretty good carrot.

Finding foundations

We return now to our passage in Romans, where Paul continues: *"and hope does not put us to shame, because God's love has been poured into our hearts through the Holy Spirit who has been given to us."*[12] Why would hope put us to shame? It would put us to shame if it failed us. Indeed, if we put our hope in God, and in the end He was unable or unwilling to do all that He had promised, other people would have good reason to mock and shame us. Maybe this is partly why we find some Christian's hesitant to hope for good things. You hear phrases such as 'I dare not hope' because they don't want to risk being

12. Rom 5:5

disappointed. Solomon in the book of Proverbs counselled his readers that "Hope deferred makes the heart sick"[13]. I know what he means, I doubt that there is anyone who hasn't experienced this; having your expectations raised so high, with your heart open and ready to receive what you've desired for so long. Then it doesn't happen. It gets delayed again, and again, and you get to a stage where you don't want to hope anymore because of the pain it's caused you. Let me say right now that God wants you to have hope. To know this great and uplifting gift, and to let it play a key role in defining you. Hope may be more than mere optimism, but that's not to say that it doesn't have that kind of effect in you. God wants to free you from the pessimism that so easily invades and drags us down. More than that – pessimism makes a comfortable couch for us to sit in and safely moan from. It's this comfort factor that in part makes it so hard to break free from. The other main factor is this fear that in turn we wrap around ourselves like a warm blanket, whilst sat in a dull self-confined space. It can be so incredibly hard to motivate yourself to break free from this situation. These self-made chains can feel so snuggly, but chains they undeniably are. But this is not the fullness of life that God has called you to, or that Christ died to give you.

13. Proverbs 13:12

So how do we nurture a hope that brings life to our fragile souls, and neither makes our hearts sick or leads us to feel shame. Well, this is another one of the great works of the Holy Spirit – something that He delights to do in us. The Spirit is responsible for bringing about the Bible as we have it. He has worked through many different people with different personalities and situations, over many, many years. With gleeful pleasure, He takes the truths contained within it and makes them alive and active in our minds. And so, to establish this hope securely, God pours His love into our hearts through the Holy Spirit, by making the truth of what Christ has done for us ring with such incredible, overwhelming love. You see at just the right time; Christ died for the ungodly – that's you and me. And therefore, He did it when we were His enemies. It's rare enough for someone to die for a friend, but to purposefully die to save your enemies is something else entirely.[14] How much more can we depend on the love of God now we're 'in Christ', adopted into God's family and treated as co-heirs with Jesus Himself.[15] Or as Paul puts it; *"how much more, now that we are reconciled, shall we be saved by his life"*.[16] And again; *"He who did not spare His own Son but gave Him up for us all, how will He not also with Him graciously give us all things?"*[17]. What is there now that can separate you

14. Rom 5:6-8
15. Rom 8:15-17
16. Rom 5:10
17. Rom 8:32

from the love of God? Can trials, distress, persecution, famine, nakedness, danger or the sword? Of course not[18]. So whatever your situation you can be sure of your loving position before God. He gave the greatest gift to you as an enemy, so you can be sure He's not going to abandon you now He's made you family. You have every reason to have hope in God.

This is not to say that you should expect every aspect of life to go smoothly and that from now on everything is going to go your way because God loves you. There has been far too much teaching along those lines in different places, and it can only lead to disappointment, disillusionment, despair or denial because it's just not true and is not what the Bible teaches at all. Amongst all these encouragements about God's love, there is also plenty of talk about suffering in different forms. And notice that it doesn't say that God's love will separate and keep you from trials, distress, persecution, famine, nakedness, danger and the sword. But rather that these things won't separate you from His love. He won't abandon you in them, and their presence doesn't mean He doesn't love you anymore. Indeed, it may be more that you've been counted worthy to endure them for His sake?[19] Which is utterly

---

18. Rom 8:35
19. Acts 5:41, 2 Thes 1:4-5

amazing, but sadly not the way that most of us tend to look at it.

Little words

Sometimes it's the little words that carry such importance, and it's worth taking a moment to note the difference between hoping *for*, and hoping *in*. As Christian's, we put our hope *in* God. As we've already considered; God is unchanging, and totalling dependable. He is all-powerful and all-knowing, so can't be overcome by force or the intelligence of another person. He is also of perfect character, and will never lie, go back on His word or be unfaithful in any way. He has a love for us so strong, that He gave His greatest gift to us whilst we were still His enemies, and through His only Son made us who believe in Him into His family through adoption. Therefore, our hope *in* God is utterly, unbreakably secure. There will always be reason to have hope, because there is always God. Even if we came to a place where all is lost and we face a hideous death, we know that God Himself awaits us on the other side. Death is not the end for a Christian. Or rather, death is only the end of all that was bad. We know we'll be resurrected with new bodies, like Christ's new body[20] no longer with any entanglement to sin, or fear of facing death again. Finally, fully, free. This is where we have certainty.

Now, what we hope *for* often doesn't carry such certainty. We may hope for God to remove an illness of obstacle from our lives. Or on a more positive note, that God will help us get that job, achieve that goal, win that competition. And there are so many great examples and testimonies of what God has done in people's lives. Many healed, impossible situations turned on their heads, forgiveness being found and love shared between former enemies. The financial means found in unexpected ways to achieve goals and help others. But there are also many examples of things not going to plan, of hopes painfully ended. So often what we hope *for* eludes us, maybe just for a while, maybe for many, many years, or perhaps it will never be. It was never wrong to hope *for* these things; the problem only arises when we place our hope *in* them. When we do this, we're making it so that our hope, our expectation of future good, is dependent on that thing or that person. So for example, you may have been desperate for a certain someone to ask you out, or for them to say yes if you ask them out. If this goes wrong, it's heart-breaking regardless. But if all your hope was *in* a possible relationship with that person, instead of hoping *for* that relationship, your

20.   Php 3:20-21

loss is even greater. As far as you can see that's it, and the whole world has ended as far as you're concerned! If you haven't experienced this, you've most likely at least seen it happen with others? Their life is of course not over, it just seems like it from their perspective, and time will show them otherwise.

God wants you to expect good things to happen, you're His child and He loves you dearly. But like any good parent that doesn't mean He'll give you whatever you want whenever you want it. There are so many things at play that we simply don't yet understand, and will not in this life. By placing our hope *in* Him, whenever things go wrong and what we hope *for* doesn't come to pass, we'll find that this God-centred hope at the core of our souls is undented and undiminished because its source has not changed or weakened. God is still the same awesome God, who works all things for ultimate good for those who know and love Him.[21]

Hope's function

It's funny in a way, suffering leads to hope, and it's hope that plays such a big role in helping us through suffering. Hope toughens you up for trials and enables trials to toughen you up. But we're doing

21. Php 3:20-21

ourselves a disservice if we only regard it as something to help us when things aren't going well. If that was its only role, then it wouldn't be relevant in the life to come, where there will be no more pain and suffering. So what does hope actually do? For a start, it helps us feel both lighter and stronger. It lifts our sights and our spirits, whilst also strengthening our souls and determination. It keeps us holding on and looking forward in the bad times, and keeps us looking up and moving forward in the good times. God wants a people who are expecting to see Him do good and great things, and hope is His great gift to embed this attitude in us.

Love, we're told is the greatest of these. I believe we can, in turn, say that Faith, is the foundation of these. And perhaps the best description we can give here, is to say that Hope, is the lifter of these. Hope lifts our sight to God, to remember what He's done, see what He is like, and remember what He has promised. In turn, this frees our souls to soar! Hope lifts them up to see a view beyond the troubles, to see an end to pain and a God who is able to rescue and make all things work for good. Hope lifts our strength and resolve, enables us to stand and stay faithful to our faithful God no matter what happens in this life. Hope lifts our sights to dream great dreams, and strive forwards exploring new things

God has for us instead of just finding a comfortable spot to stay. It lifts us up not just to endure hard times, but to keep moving and pursuing God in the good times. Hope is a wonderful and often undervalued gift of God. We need to learn to cherish and cultivate it.

Fear can hold you prisoner

You may have seen what is now a fairly old film: The Shawshank Redemption? I along with many others love this film. It's a real shame that there's so much bad language in it, certainly in the early parts of the film, but it's worth pushing through with, and I know no better film about hope. The film brilliantly depicts the difference hope can make in someone's life, or indeed its absence. There's a tag line never used in the film, but that appeared on the posters: *"Fear can hold you prisoner; Hope can set you free."* There's a lot of truth in that, and although it's probably faith that's the biggest weapon against fear, it's hope that is fear's opposite. For surely a good definition of fear is: 'the expectation of future bad'?

So as we draw this book to a close, let's consider two sad stories where fear held people back, held them captive and caused them to miss out on what

God had for them. In this, we will see the contrast of being motivated by fear or by hope. Indeed, in these two cases, we should really say faith and hope, for rarely are any of our core three motivators operating on their own.

The Promised Land

Our first story is from the Old Testament, the Israelites have been rescued from slavery in Egypt, and have been spending time getting to know God and His requirements of them. The law has been given, the Levitical Priesthood established, and all this while God has been miraculously providing for their needs; manna from heaven, water from rocks, battles won, and even the simple fact that neither their clothes nor their sandals have worn out during this time (and neither will they until they're in the promised land)[22]. Now they're finally preparing to enter and conquer the promised land, so on the Lord's command spies are sent, twelve in total, and after forty days they returned with their report: *"We went into the land to which you sent us, and it does flow with milk and honey! Here is its fruit. But the people who live there are powerful, and the cities are fortified and very large. We even saw descendants of*

22. Deut 29:5

Anak there… But the men who had gone up with him said, 'We can't attack those people; they are stronger than we are.' And they spread among the Israelites a bad report about the land they had explored. They said, 'The land we explored devours those living in it. All the people we saw there are of great size.'[23]

They saw two things very clearly; first, that the land was as good as promised – there was no hype, God was as good as His word and it does indeed flow with milk and honey, a beautiful and fertile land. Secondly, they saw that the opposition was strong, very strong. With large fortified cities, and indeed large fort-like people, giants. They would later go on to compare themselves as being grasshoppers in comparison. But don't let this obvious exaggeration deceive you – the people in the land were strong, indeed *some* may have even been 'giants', even if nowhere near as big as they suggested (think more along the lines of Goliath who was around nine feet, or a little under three metres!). But they failed to see one thing. God.

It is unwise to go into a situation without knowing what you're facing – both the rewards and the challenges. But how much more foolish is it when we don't trust God and take Him at His word. By now, God had repeatedly revealed His power, His ability to sustain and to look after the Israelites, and

23. Num 13:27-28;31-32

the spies had now seen with their own eyes that God does not exaggerate (He is always true) – the land was as good as He had promised. But this is not where their eyes held their focus, and so fear took the place of faith and hope. The result? Infection. A whole nation was persuaded by the fear of ten spies, that the job of conquering the land was too hard and could not be done. They rebelled against God and would have stoned Moses along with the few people who stood by him in this matter, had God not intervened[24]. His response is a sobering one. At first, He threatens to wipe out the people and start again building a nation out of Moses and his descendants. But Moses intercedes, and pleading for God's own namesake among the other nations[25], God agrees to spare the people (don't ever think that prayer doesn't make a difference). Nonetheless, there are still consequences: *"The LORD replied, "I have forgiven them, as you asked. Nevertheless, as surely as I live and as surely as the glory of the LORD fills the whole earth, not one of the men who saw my glory and the miraculous signs I performed in Egypt and in the desert but who disobeyed me and tested me ten times - not one of them will ever see the land I promised on oath to their forefathers. No one who has treated me with contempt will ever see it."*[26]

---

24. Num 14:10
25. Num 14:11-19
26. Num 14:20-23 NIV

Sobering. Forgiveness is sought and found for the people, but fear has held them back from following God and entering the land He promised to them. Fear has led them to treat God with contempt, and so they'll live out the rest of their lives in a wilderness. Fear can indeed hold you prisoner.

Gerasenes

Our next sad story is found in the New Testament, just after Jesus calms a storm by simply commanding it. He and His disciples have now sailed from Galilee to the other side of the lake to the country of the Gerasenes. There near the shore, Jesus encounters a man who had long been plagued by a 'Legion' of demons. At times this man had been kept under guard by the locals, chained and shackled, but he would break his bonds and be driven by the demons into the desert to live naked among the tombs. But this is not the saddest bit of the story. Upon seeing Jesus, the demons within the man know their time is up, and curiously ask to be sent into a nearby herd of pigs. Equally curiously Jesus allows this, and the demons leave the man, enter the pigs, causing them all to go rushing down into the lake and drown. A dramatic event to be sure, which is witnessed by the pig's herdsmen who go and tell the nearby city. Now, this is where we hit the truly sad part: "*...and the people went out to see what had happened. When they came to Jesus, they found the man from whom the demons had gone out, sitting at Jesus' feet, dressed and in his right mind; and they were afraid. Those who had seen it told the people how the demon-possessed man had been cured. Then all the people of the region of the Gerasenes asked Jesus to leave them, because they were overcome with fear. So he got into the boat and left.*"[27].

This story kind of breaks my heart. In the last one we see fear taking hold because the people *couldn't* see that God was with them, and the complete difference He makes to a situation. In this story, fear took hold of them because they *could* see God at work and the difference He was already making. Once again, instead of faith and hope rising in their hearts, fear took their rightful/helpful place, and they asked Him to leave. So He did. No fuss, no trying to argue or reason with them. They had been visited by the God-man, Jesus Christ, who had done a wonderful work and set a man free from a horror I can barely begin to appreciate. Why? Why did this give birth to fear? We can be so easily afraid of change and the unknown, the powerful and uncontrollable. Jesus represented all these things to

27. Luke 8:35-37 NIV

them immediately. He'd only just arrived, but already He's changed and rescued a man they could not help or tame. He'd shown great authority, speaking to and commanding demons to leave, and they obeyed, for they had no choice. Jesus was obviously like no man they had ever encountered before, and they simply did not know what to make of Him.

When God is at work, it can sometimes get a little scary. Out of the ordinary things can happen, and even though they're wonderful acts to bless people in different ways, they can make you feel very vulnerable and out of control. Indeed, you're *not* fully in control. In turn, you can let fear put up a shield around you to "protect" yourself from what's going on, and sure enough, God will pass you by. But some time later you will find that it was no shield, but rather a cage of your own making, which prevented you from stepping into all that God wants to give and do in/through you. Fear can hold you prisoner.

There's another possibility. Maybe it was about the cost? They had just lost around two thousand pigs![28] That would be a lot to lose now, I presume it would be much more significant in those days. So Christ's presence had already cost them substantially – what might be the price if He stayed? Following Christ will always involve cost, and you should have no doubts and no surprises about this. Jesus was quite

28. Mark 5:13

clear: *"And whoever does not carry their cross and follow me cannot be my disciple. Suppose one of you wants to build a tower. Won't you first sit down and estimate the cost to see if you have enough money to complete it? For if you lay the foundation and are not able to finish it, everyone who sees it will ridicule you, saying, "This person began to build and wasn't able to finish" ... In the same way, those of you who do not give up everything you have cannot be my disciples."*[29]

What does it cost to follow Christ? Everything. That is to say, you must surrender everything to Him, your whole life and all that you have. You may or may not be called upon to actually give it all up, but our attitude must be at a place where we'd be willing to, where it's no longer just ours but His. To believe and follow Christ Jesus means to fully submit to Him. *"You are not your own, for you were bought with a price"*[30]. Such a cost, such a surrender, can be a scary thing, and it's easy to see how fear could find a way in here. But as a friend of mine likes to say: "You can't out-give God." And he's right. Whatever God asks or demands of us is for our good. There is nothing given to God (if given rightly) that won't be paid back many times over. Not because He is then in your debt, far from it - we owe everything to Him

---

29. Luke 14:27-30;33
30. 1 Cor 6:19-20

eternally, but because He delights to do this. As John Ortberg In his book 'The Me I Want To Be' says:

> *"On the other side of death is freedom, and no one is more free than a dead man. Jesus had much to say about death to self, and on the journey to the me you want to be, you'll have some dying to do. But that kind of death is always death to a lesser self, a false self, so that a better and nobler self can come to life."*[31]

So let us do the math and count the cost. What is this cost? Everything, our very lives included. What's the reward? More. Knowing and being with God Himself, and fullness of life in ways we cannot imagine (but that shouldn't stop us trying). If you let fear shackle you and hold you back from surrendering anything or everything to Christ, you will lose out. Fear will hold you prisoner, and in turn rob you blind.

Hope can set you free

As sad as these two stories are, they aren't without the seeds of hope either. Forty years later the

---

31. John Ortberg, The Me I Want To Be, P26, 2010

Israelites would return, with the old generation who treated God with contempt having all passed away. Just two remained Joshua, and Caleb, the only spies who came back having seen exactly the same things, but who also saw God for who He is. They had remained faithful and tried but failed to persuade the others that they could conquer the promised land because God was with them. It must have been a frustrating forty years waiting, but their hope did not diminish and return they did. This time with a new generation, with eyes of faith and hope, ready to follow God and claim His promise to them. As for the man freed from demons at Gerasenes – he wanted to leave that place with Jesus. But Jesus told him to return home and declare all that God had done for him. Which he did, throughout the whole city.[32] Who but God knows what ground-work that man did in preparing the people of that city to hear the gospel of Jesus Christ; His life, death and resurrection? A seed was planted there that day, and I'm sure God made it grow and bear fruit.

Is there any area of your life where fear is holding you back?

- Fear will focus on the fact that you could be hurt. Hope will remind you that Jesus suffered in so

32. Luke 8:38-39

many, and such extreme ways. And that even if you are hurt, you have a God of peace and comfort, who is worth hurting for.
- Fear will focus on the potential pain of rejection. Hope will remind you that Jesus was rejected, even by those closest to Him. But He will never abandon you.
- Fear tells you that you're not good enough, that it could go horribly wrong, and you will look like a fool. Hope will remind you that God loves you and excepts you before you even begin. That He will be with you, and that we could never do it without Him anyway.
- Fear will focus on the potential of failing. Hope will remind you how God works good through all things including your failures.

And of course, hope lets you see that anything could go far better than you can even imagine. It frees you not just to know that God can do wonderful things, but more than this – to *expect* God to do good and great things. *Fear can hold you prisoner; Hope will set you free.*

Daydreaming with God

> *"...no eye has seen, nor ear heard, nor the heart of man imagined, what God has prepared for those who love him"*
>
> *1 Cor 2:9*

Let me leave you with a final thought that has long intrigued me. In 1 Cor 13:13 Pauls says that *"faith, hope, and love abide…"* Here in context, he's contrasting the Spiritual gifts and these three virtues saying that whereas the gifts will pass away in the life to come, faith, hope and love will all remain as significant and of great value forever. Now love's continuing role is immediately easy to see and understand, but what about faith and hope? Do we still need faith (being certain of what we don't see) when we'll be able to see God face to face? Do we still need hope (the expectation of future good) when we've finally arrived at our ultimate and awesome future promised to us? What's the significance of these still being an important part of us? I can only speculate of course, but here's what I think may be the implication – activity. It's easy to think of the next life as one big and eternal retirement home. Certainly, that's what has come across to me at times when I've heard it spoken about? And of course, there are all those pictures out there of people floating around on clouds, maybe playing an instrument. Indeed, that's another possibility sometimes inferred – that eternity will be one long worship session. And while it's true that our future life will indeed be full of praising God, it's worth remembering that Paul, speaking to the church in Rome, spoke of our spiritual act of worship being in the way that we live and use our bodies (a living sacrifice).[33] The ways in which we praise God then will be no doubt even richer and more varied than the ways we worship Him now. If I'm honest, none of these previous things mentioned has filled me with much eagerness or anticipation for our future life with God. Any singular thing done forever without end, however good it may be, ultimately fills me with weariness, if not dread. Admittedly this is probably not a great reaction inside of me, but it is the honest one. However, considering faith and hope continuing on through all time, starts to awaken my soul. That surely indicates, activity, discovery and growth? No longer with any fear or strife in the background, or battling against evil in any form, but rather an enduring life of discovering God, and His creativeness. Of exploring new things, and learning. Of stepping out into the new with absolute faith, without even the slightest hint of fear in the background. Of a life where there is always

33. Rom 12:1

something to look forward to, as well as fully appreciating what you already have and experience. A life where we will never exhaust the wonder, playfulness and imagination of our God.

We simply cannot imagine what God has in store for us. But that doesn't mean we shouldn't try. It just means whatever we can come up with in our puny minds will be utterly exceeded by the reality. So I invite you to do some 'daydreaming' with God. Ponder it, ask Him about it. Search the scriptures for what it does say about it (for some details are given). Then sit back and let your excitement grow for our future life with God, endeavouring to live now in the light of then.

> *"May the God of hope fill you with all joy and peace in believing, so that by the power of the Holy Spirit you may abound in hope."*
>
> Romans 15:13

Other books in this series:

Faith's Motive:

Faith goes beyond mere belief, even demons know about the one true God. Faith runs deeper and takes you further, constantly affirming to your soul – God is Greater!

Faith is the foundation of these.

Other books in this series:

Love's Motive:

Neither merely a feeling nor simply a choice that you make. Love is a motive and the way in which we place true value in other people. Sourced and sustained in God, the beauty of this gift defies description, yet inspires us to try.

Love is the greatest of these.

www.ingramcontent.com/pod-product-compliance
Lightning Source LLC
Chambersburg PA
CBHW071547080526
44588CB00011B/1819